My First Bible in Pictures   PRESENTED TO

Esther Marygrace Gordon

BY

Aunt Gwen & Uncle Joe

ON

Your 2nd Birthday

I have long loved
the Bible illustrations
by Richard and Frances
Hook. I hope you will love
them, also.

My First Bible
IN PICTURES

~ *15th Anniversary Edition* ~

With millions of copies in over 60 languages
worldwide, *My First Bible in Pictures* has met
the spiritual needs of children all over the globe.
Its mission was to bring Bible stories to children
in a way they would understand—simple words
and compelling pictures. With excitement,
Tyndale House Publishers is now celebrating
with this 15th Anniversary Edition.
We want to thank you for making this
a family classic.

~

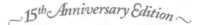

~15th Anniversary Edition~

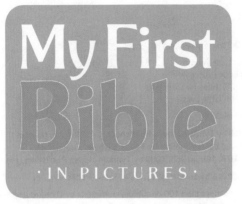

My First Bible

·IN PICTURES·

Kenneth N. Taylor

with illustrations by
Richard and Frances Hook

Tyndale House Publishers, Inc.
CAROL STREAM, ILLINOIS

Other Children's Books by Kenneth N. Taylor

Big Thoughts for Little People
Good News for Little People
The New Bible in Pictures for Little Eyes
Jesus in Pictures for Little Eyes

My First Bible in Pictures

Copyright © 1989 by Tyndale House Publishers, Inc. All rights reserved.
Text © 1989 owned by assignment by Tyndale House Foundation.
Illustrations © 1976, 1985, 1988, 1989 by Tyndale House Publishers, Inc.

Tyndale Kids logo is a trademark of Tyndale House Publishers, Inc.

This book contains more than 100 beautiful illustrations by Richard and Frances Hook.
Tyndale House gratefully acknowledges the following publishers for permission to print
their Hook art:

Concordia Publishing House: The Hook illlustrations on pages 43, 135, 157, 169, 187, 191,
205, 223, 233 and 235 are taken from *My Good Shepherd Bible Story Book,* copyright 1969
by Concordia Publishing House, St. Louis, MO 63118, and are used by permission.

The Standard Publishing Company: The Hook illustrations on pages 77 and 245 are taken
from *Frances Hook Picture Book,* copyright 1963, 1964 by The Standard Publishing
Company, Cincinnati, OH 45231, and are used by permission.

Other artists:

Ron Ferris: pages 7, 11, 15, 19, 27, 95, 109, 115, 121, 127, 155, 221, 253.

Corbert Gauthier: pages 37, 41, 57, 59, 69, 89, 91, 105, 117, 141, 203.

Janice Skivington Wood: page 255.

Printed in Colombia

Library of Congress Catalog Card Number 89-50692

ISBN-13: 978-0-8423-4633-7	ISBN-10: 0-8423-4633-3 Red
ISBN-13: 978-0-8423-4630-6	ISBN-10: 0-8423-4630-9 Red Handled Edition
ISBN-13: 978-1-4143-0592-9	ISBN-10: 1-4143-0592-3 Blue
ISBN-13: 978-1-4143-0593-6	ISBN-10: 1-4143-0593-1 Pink

12 11 10
29 28 27

A Note to Parents

This is a "carry-to-church" book of Bible stories for little people. But don't leave it on the shelf during the week. Read it with your children at home. The stories and illustrations introduce children to the great people of the Bible. The important themes of the Bible will be planted in little lives, to grow there throughout a lifetime. Above all, the stories tell about God and his Son Jesus, and about God's demand for truth and righteousness.

Many of the stories have obvious applications for young children. A simple question brings home the truth of each story, helping to anchor important facts in children's minds.

For many, many years I have been writing to help children grow in the grace of God. I hope this book, doubtless one of my final efforts, will accomplish its purpose in your children's lives. May God bless each one of them in a special way.

Kenneth N. Taylor

God made the whole world. He made the flowers and the trees and the water and the stars. God made the sun so we can have daylight. The sun makes us warm when we are outside on sunny days. Thank you, God, for making the sun.

Who made the sun?

GENESIS 1

Adam and Eve were the very first man and woman. God made them. He gave them a beautiful place to live called the Garden of Eden. They were very happy. God made the animals, too. Point to the elephant. Where is the zebra?

Who made Adam and Eve?

GENESIS 1–2

Adam and Eve are sorry and sad. They did something God told them not to do. Now God is punishing them. They must go away from their nice home in the Garden of Eden. The angels won't let them go back.

Why must Adam and Eve leave their nice home?

GENESIS 3

Adam and Eve had two sons.
Their names are Cain and Abel.
Abel obeyed God, but Cain did not
obey God. Cain was angry and
killed Abel. This was wrong.
Adam and Eve were very sad. God
was sad, too.

*What are the names of Adam and
Eve's sons?*

GENESIS 4

God told Noah to build a huge boat. It is called an ark. Noah's sons are helping him. The ark is not in the water. But soon it will begin to rain and rain until there is water everywhere. Noah and all his family will be safe in the boat.

Where will Noah and his family be when it rains?

GENESIS 6

Noah finished building the boat. Then God told him to bring two of each kind of animal and bird into the boat. There are two giraffes and two tigers and two ducks. They will all be safe in the ark when the flood comes.

How many kangaroos are there?

GENESIS 7

It rained and rained and rained. Soon everything was covered with water. But Noah's boat is floating on the water. Yes, God took care of Noah and his family and the animals in the boat. God takes care of you, too.

Who is in the boat?

GENESIS 7

The people are building a big tower. It is called the Tower of Babel. The people think they can build it up to heaven. But God doesn't want them to build the tower. He will make them stop. Suddenly they won't understand each other's words!

Who made the people stop building the tower?

GENESIS 11

Abraham was a special friend of God. His wife is Sarah. God told Abraham to move to another country. God said he would give Abraham the entire country for his family to live in forever. Abraham has many sheep and donkeys. Can you point to them?

What is the man's name? What is his wife's name?

GENESIS 12

Abraham and his wife Sarah were very sad because they didn't have any children. But who is this big boy? Now they have a son. His name is Isaac. They are happy because God answered their prayer and gave them a son.

What is the name of Abraham and Sarah's son?

When Isaac grew up, he married Rebekah and had a son named Jacob. Jacob was tired and went to sleep with his head on a rock for a pillow! He had a dream about angels going up and down from heaven. Then God told Jacob, "I will take care of you."

What did Jacob dream about?

GENESIS 28

Jacob had a twin brother named Esau. When the boys grew up, they had a big argument. Jacob moved far away. Finally he sent a message to Esau. He said he hoped they could be friends again. Now they are happy to see each other.

What are the names of the brothers?

GENESIS 33

The old man is Jacob. He has twelve sons. He loves his son Joseph very much. He gave Joseph a beautiful coat. Joseph's brothers are angry because their father didn't give them nice coats, too. They should be happy for Joseph.

What did Joseph's father give him?

GENESIS 37

This baby's name is Moses.
The young woman is a princess.
She found the baby in a basket in
a river. Bad men wanted to kill
the baby. God sent the princess to
find the baby Moses and take care
of him.

Where did the princess find the baby Moses?

EXODUS 2

Now Moses has become a big man. One day he saw a bush on fire, but it didn't burn up! God spoke to Moses from the bush. God said, "Go and help my people." Moses was afraid at first, but God said, "I will help you."

What did God tell Moses to do?

EXODUS 3

God's people are living in Egypt. The man with the whip is telling them to work harder. They will ask God to help them. God will send Moses to make the man stop hurting them. Moses will help all of God's people.

Who will help God's people?

EXODUS 5

Moses told Pharaoh to let God's people move away from Egypt. Pharaoh said no. God sent many flies and frogs and other problems to bother the Egyptians. Pharaoh still said no. Finally God said he would kill the oldest boy in each family in Egypt.

What did Moses tell Pharaoh?

EXODUS 7–11

Moses told God's people to put blood above their doors and beside their doors. God would not kill anyone in the house if he saw blood at the door. The night this happened is called the Passover. Finally Pharaoh said God's people could leave Egypt. They left that night.

Why is there blood above the door?

EXODUS 12

God's people are walking along the bottom of a big lake called the Red Sea. Can you see the water standing up along both sides? When Moses held up his stick, God made the water open up. Now the people can walk on dry ground through the lake.

Who made the water open up?

EXODUS 14

This family is picking up little pieces of bread. God sent the bread down from heaven so his people would not be hungry. God fed his people this way every morning. Point to the little girl who is saying thank you to God.

Where did the bread come from?

EXODUS 16

God's people were very thirsty, but they didn't have anything to drink. God told Moses to hit the rock with his stick. When he did this, God made water come out of the rock. Then everyone could have a big drink.

What happened when Moses hit the rock with his stick?

EXODUS 17

Moses is listening to God. God is telling Moses ten very important rules he wants his people to obey. God wrote these ten rules on pieces of stone. These rules are called the Ten Commandments.

What are God's ten rules called?

EXODUS 20

Oh, no! See what God's people are doing! They made an idol that looks like a calf. They are worshipping the idol instead of worshipping God. This made God angry and sad. God had to punish them for doing this.

What are these people doing? Why is this bad?

EXODUS 31–32

This beautiful tent is called the Tabernacle. It was God's house. People came here to say thank you to God and to pray to him. The people worshipped God in the Tabernacle. It was their church.

Does the Tabernacle look like your church?

EXODUS 35–36

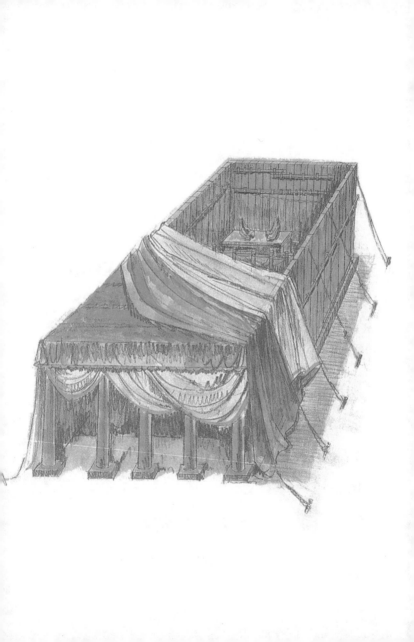

Moses is leading the people on a long trip. How does Moses know where to go? He is looking up to watch a special cloud that God put there. Moses and the people follow wherever God moves the cloud. Can you point to the cloud?

Who is moving the cloud?

EXODUS 40

Look at the big bunch of grapes these men are carrying! The men's names are Caleb and Joshua. The grapes grew in the country God promised to give to his people. The men are hurrying home to show their friends what good things grow in the Promised Land.

Where did these grapes grow?

NUMBERS 13–14

Snakes were biting God's people, and some of the people died. God told Moses to make something that looked like a big snake. The people who were bitten could look up at the snake on the pole. Then God made them well again.

Who made the people well again?

NUMBERS 21

God didn't want Balaam to go down this road. So God sent an angel to stop him. When the donkey saw the angel, it stopped. Balaam hit the donkey to make it go again. Then the donkey talked! It asked, "Why did you hit me?" Finally Balaam saw the angel and was glad the donkey stopped!

What did the donkey say?

Joshua was the next leader of God's people. God told him to destroy the town of Jericho. Joshua and all the people walked around the walls and blew their trumpets and shouted. Now all the walls are falling down so God's people can go in.

What is happening to the walls?

JOSHUA 6

Gideon wanted to take ten thousand soldiers with him to fight God's enemies. God wanted him to take only a few. God told Gideon to choose only the three hundred men who drank from their hands. Gideon was afraid to have such a small army, but God said he would help him.

How many soldiers did Gideon take?

JUDGES 7

Samson was a very, very strong man. See how easily he broke the ropes! Once he killed a lion with his bare hands. Another time he knocked down a palace to punish God's enemies. God made him strong so he could help God's people.

What is the man's name?

JUDGES 15

The man in the white robe is Job (his name rhymes with *robe*). He was a good man who always tried to do what God said. Then Satan asked God to let terrible things happen to Job. Job was very sad, but he still loved God.

Did Job always love God?

JOB 1

The lady in blue is Naomi. She is sad because her husband and sons have died. Ruth is trying to help Naomi feel better. She will stay with Naomi. God wants us to be helpers, too. What can you do to help someone?

What is the name of the woman who is helping Naomi?

RUTH 1

amuel was only a little boy, but he lived at the Tabernacle and helped Eli the priest. One night he heard a voice calling his name. At first he thought it was Eli. But it was God's voice. God had a message for Samuel. Samuel listened to God and obeyed.

Who was calling Samuel?

1 SAMUEL 2

After Samuel grew up, God's people wanted a king. God was not happy about this. He knew there would be problems. But he chose Saul to be the king. Saul was tall and handsome. Samuel tells the people, "Here is your new king. Obey him."

Who became the king?

1 SAMUEL 8

David was a special friend of God. When he was a boy he took care of his father's sheep. Can you see his harp beside him? He wrote beautiful songs to tell God that he loved him. Many of his songs are in the Bible. They are called the Psalms.

What did David write?

1 SAMUEL 16

This lion wants to eat David's sheep. Can you point to the lion? Where are the sheep? God has made David strong and brave. With God's help David will kill the lion so it can't hurt the sheep.

Will the lion hurt the sheep? Why not?

1 SAMUEL 17

Goliath wants to hurt God's people with his spear and sword. David is using his slingshot to throw a stone at Goliath. David knows God will help him. The stone will hit Goliath on his face and Goliath will fall down, dead. God's people will be safe.

Who killed Goliath?

1 SAMUEL 17

King Saul had a son named Jonathan. David and Jonathan were best friends. But King Saul wanted to kill David. Jonathan helped David hide from the king. Jonathan knew he must obey God and help David even if his father said he should not do this. You and I must always obey God, too.

Who was David's friend?

1 SAMUEL 20

It is night, and King Saul is asleep. He has been trying to find David to kill him. David has been hiding, but now he sees King Saul. Should David hurt the king? God does not want him to hurt King Saul. David will obey God.

Did David hurt the king?

1 SAMUEL 26

amuel is old now, but he is still one of God's helpers. God told him to pour olive oil on David's head. This is how God showed everyone that David would become the next king of God's people. God will help David be a good king.

Who would be the new king of God's people?

1 SAMUEL 16

Now David is the king of
Israel. The big golden box behind
him is called the Ark of the
Covenant. He is bringing the Ark
to Jerusalem. He is jumping for
joy. He loves God and God loves
him. God loves you, too. You
should be very happy.

Why is King David so happy?

2 SAMUEL 6

This beautiful woman is Bath-sheba. King David did something very wrong. He killed Bath-sheba's husband so he could marry her. When he did this, David broke some of God's most important rules. This made God very angry, so he punished David.

Why was God angry with David?

2 SAMUEL 11–12

This is King David's son Absalom. The king's soldiers were chasing him because he did not obey the king. Absalom was riding on his donkey under the tree. His hair got caught in the branches, and his donkey left him hanging there. Then King David's army found him.

What happened to Absalom's hair?

2 SAMUEL 18

David has another son named Solomon. God's helper, Nathan, is putting his hands on Solomon's head to make him the next king. Solomon asked God to make him a wise king. God was pleased with Solomon and gave him great wisdom.

What did Solomon ask God to give him?

1 KINGS 1

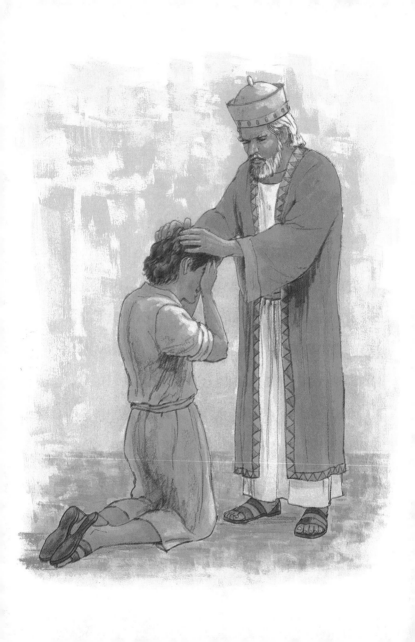

These two women are fighting over the baby. Each says the baby is hers. God made King Solomon know which woman was really the baby's mother. He gave the baby back to its mother. Then everyone thanked God for giving them such a wise king.

Why were the women arguing?

1 KINGS 3

King Solomon built a
beautiful church for God called
the Temple. Can you see him
standing there? He is thanking
God. The king is very happy
because he is God's helper. You
and I can be God's helpers, too.
This will make God happy.

What did King Solomon build?

1 KINGS 8

King Solomon is breaking one of God's most important rules. Do you know what he is doing wrong? He is praying to these animals made of gold. We know he should pray only to God. God is angry with him and will send many troubles into Solomon's life.

What did Solomon do wrong?

1 KINGS 11

Elijah is God's helper. He is called a prophet. Elijah is very hungry. He loves God, so God sent these birds to bring him food. Can you see the bread the birds are bringing him? God is taking care of him. God takes care of you, too. *What did the birds bring to Elijah?*

1 KINGS 17

Elijah asked God to send fire from heaven. Can you point to Elijah? He has his hands lifted to God. Elijah is showing that God is very powerful. Did God answer Elijah's prayer? Yes! Look at the fire God sent!

What did God send from heaven?

1 KINGS 18

What is happening here? God has sent horses made of fire and a chariot made of fire to take Elijah up to heaven! No one has seen Elijah again. He is in heaven with God. Elisha will be the new prophet

What are the horses made of?
Where did God take Elijah?

2 KINGS 2

The only food this lady had was some olive oil in a jar. God's new helper, Elisha, told her to pour her oil into many other jars. She poured and poured, but her jar didn't get empty! Now she can sell the jars of olive oil and buy food.

How did Elisha help the woman?

2 KINGS 4

This lady is Elisha's friend.
One day her little boy became ill and
died. The mother ran to Elisha and
asked him to help. Elisha prayed,
and the boy came back to life! The
boy's parents were glad. God can
do anything!

What happened to the boy?

2 KINGS 4

The man in the chariot is sick. The little girl told him that God's helper, Elisha, could make him well. Naaman is going away in his chariot to visit Elisha. When Elisha prayed, God made Naaman well.

What did the girl tell the sick man?

Can you see the tree on the ground? These young men were chopping it with axes. One man's axe fell into the river, and it sank to the bottom. But Elisha, God's helper, told the axe to float. Now the man can have it again.

What happened to the man's axe?

2 KINGS 6

These people are happy. They are singing and playing on horns and drums as they walk to their church. They are telling God, "Thank you for helping us." You and I can thank God, too. We can bow our heads and close our eyes and say, "Thank you, God."

What are these people telling God?

2 CHRONICLES 20

When Prince Joash was a baby, his wicked grandmother wanted to kill him! His uncle and aunt hid Joash until he was seven. Now he has become king! The soldiers are taking his grandmother away so she can't hurt him. Joash loves God and is a good king.

How old is Joash?

2 KINGS 11

These people are repairing their church building. King Joash knows this is the right thing to do. The people want to have a place where everyone can thank God for all the kind things he does for them.

What would you like to thank God for?

2 KINGS 12

Jonah didn't want to obey God. He tried to run away on a boat, but God sent a storm. Jonah was thrown into the water. The big fish swallowed him. After three days the fish spit Jonah out onto the sand. Now Jonah will obey God.

What happened to Jonah?

JONAH 1–2

King Ahaz is a bad king. He is telling the men to nail the church doors shut. He doesn't want anyone to go in and pray to God. God will punish him for doing this. Aren't you glad that no one has nailed your church doors shut?

What is happening to the church doors?

2 CHRONICLES 28

Many of the kings of God's people worshipped idols. They taught God's people to pray to the idols. They asked the idols to make their gardens grow. They thanked the idols for rain. This was foolish. Now King Hezekiah's men are smashing the idols and will pray only to God.

What are the men breaking?

2 KINGS 18

This man is reading God's rules to King Josiah. The king didn't know about these rules. Now he will obey them and do what God wants. We have God's rules in the Bible. When we read the Bible we can obey God and make him happy.

Where can we find God's rules?

2 KINGS 22

Jeremiah was one of God's helpers. He told the people what God wanted them to do. Some men didn't want to listen, so they put him in this deep hole. Jeremiah was brave. When they took him out, he kept on telling them what God wanted them to do.

What is this man's name?

JEREMIAH 38

The beautiful city of Jerusalem is burning. The enemies of God's people have set it on fire. Why did God let them do this? It is because the people in the city prayed to idols instead of praying to God.

What is happening to the beautiful city?

JEREMIAH 39

Daniel and his three friends are talking to the king. The king burned the city of Jerusalem where they lived. But now the king likes Daniel and his friends. The king will ask them to help him rule the kingdom.

What will the king ask Daniel and his friends to do?

DANIEL 1

The king made a big statue of himself and said everyone must pray to it. But Shadrach, Meshach, and Abednego will not pray to the statue. They will pray only to God. The king is angry and says he will punish them. But look in the next picture to see what happened!

Why are these men standing up?

DANIEL 3

The king threw Shadrach, Meshach, and Abednego into the fire because they would pray only to God. But look! There are four men in the fire! God has sent his angel to take care of them! The fire didn't hurt them at all!

Who is taking care of them in the fire?

DANIEL 3

The king is frightened. He sees a big hand. The hand is writing on the wall. The king can't read the words, but God tells Daniel what the words mean. The words say the king has been bad. God will not let him be king anymore.

What do the words on the wall say?

DANIEL 5

Daniel prayed only to God. He would not pray to the king. The king's helpers punished Daniel by putting him with hungry lions. They thought the lions would eat him. But God sent an angel to protect Daniel. The lions will not hurt him.

What happened to Daniel?

DANIEL 6

This beautiful woman is Queen Esther. She loves God and is kind to God's people. She is brave. She is telling the king to help God's people. The king is listening and will do what Queen Esther has asked him to do.

What is the queen's name?

ESTHER 5

The Temple Solomon built had
been destroyed. Now the people
have built a beautiful new Temple.
It is their church. All the people
can come and pray. God is very
pleased with his people. He wants
us to go to church and worship him.
*What is this beautiful building
called?*

EZRA 6

The angel Gabriel is telling Mary something very important. He is telling her she will be the mother of God's Son! Mary is very excited! She is happy because she will be the mother of the Saviour. She will name the baby Jesus.

What did the angel tell Mary?

LUKE 1

Zacharias and Elizabeth are so happy with their baby boy. An angel told Zacharias he would have a son and should name him John. When John grew up, he told people that Jesus was coming. You can tell your friends about Jesus, too.

What is the baby's name?

LUKE 1

This is Mary's baby. Do you remember his name? It is Jesus! He is God's Son, but he was born in a barn where sheep and donkeys live. He was a great king in heaven before he came down to earth as a baby.

Where was Jesus born?

LUKE 2

These shepherds were outside taking care of their sheep. Suddenly they saw an angel. He told them Jesus had been born in a barn in the town of Bethlehem. Now many other angels have come. They are praising God because Jesus came to save us.

What did the angel tell the shepherds?

LUKE 2

The shepherds ran into town to find the baby. They found him in a barn, just as the angel said. Mary is cuddling her baby. Jesus looked like any baby, but the shepherds knew he was God's Son. The angel had told them that Jesus is the Saviour.

Where did the shepherds find Jesus?

LUKE 2

Simeon is a very old man. He has been waiting for many years to see God's Son. Mary and Joseph have brought baby Jesus to the Temple. Now Simeon is very happy! He is thanking God for this special child. His long wait is over!

Who was Simeon waiting to see?

LUKE 2

Here is the baby Jesus and his mother, Mary. Some wise men from far away have come with presents for Jesus. They saw a star that led them to Jesus. They know Jesus will be very great and important. That is why they are bringing him gifts.

Why are they bringing gifts to Jesus?

MATTHEW 2

J oseph is taking Mary and the baby Jesus on a long trip. They are running away from some men who want to kill the baby. They are going to Egypt. God is taking care of Jesus by telling Joseph to take him far away.

Why are they taking the long trip?

MATTHEW 2

Jesus and his family have returned to their home. Now Jesus is getting bigger. He is God's Son, but he is also Mary's son. He listens carefully to Mary and Joseph as they teach him. They love him, and he loves and obeys them.

Who was Jesus' mother?

LUKE 2

Jesus has become a big boy. He is twelve years old. He is in the Temple talking to the leaders of God's people. Jesus is listening to them and asking them questions. They are all surprised at his good answers.

Why are the men surprised?

LUKE 2

Jesus has grown up and become a man. His cousin John baptized people who loved God. John has just baptized Jesus in the river. The Holy Spirit is coming down from heaven in the form of a dove. God's voice from heaven said, "Jesus is my dear Son."

What did the voice from heaven say?

LUKE 3

The man in the striped coat is Nicodemus. He is asking Jesus how to get to heaven. Jesus is telling him that anyone who believes in God's Son will go to heaven. Do you know the name of God's Son? His name is Jesus.

What is the man asking Jesus?

JOHN 3

Jesus is talking with his friends. They are called his disciples. Some of them were fishermen, but Jesus is telling them to come with him. They will tell people that God loves them. You can tell people about Jesus, too, and that you love him.

What are Jesus' helpers called?

JOHN 1

This woman came to get water from the well. Jesus told her he could give her something better than water. He could give her a happy life with God. She believed Jesus and went to tell her friends. They came and believed in Jesus, too.

What could Jesus give the woman?

JOHN 4

These men had been fishing all night. They couldn't catch any fish. Then Jesus came and told them to try once more. He made the fish go into the net. Now the men have all these fish. Jesus is very great. He can do anything.

What did Jesus make the fish do?

LUKE 5

Jesus is telling the people about God. He is saying that God wants us to be kind to everyone. He doesn't want us to quarrel or get angry. Jesus gave us the Golden Rule: "Do for others what you want them to do for you."

What can you do to help someone?

MATTHEW 5

This girl was very ill. While her father was trying to find Jesus, the girl died. Jesus came to her house and said, "Get up, little girl!" And she came back to life. You can see she is well again now. What wonderful things Jesus does.

What happened to this girl?

LUKE 8

This man was blind. Close your eyes right now and pretend you are blind. Isn't it wonderful to be able to see? "Do you believe I can make you see?" Jesus asked the man. "Yes," the man answered. Then Jesus touched his eyes, and he could see!

What do you see when you close your eyes?

MARK 8

Jesus was sleeping in the boat during a big storm. His friends were scared. They thought the boat was going to sink. They woke Jesus up. "We are all going to die," they screamed. But Jesus stood up and told the storm to go away. And it did.

What did Jesus tell the storm to do?

LUKE 8

Peter is in the water. He needs help! Jesus is coming to help him. Jesus is not sinking like Peter because Jesus is God's Son. He can even walk on top of the water! Jesus will help you, too, if you ask him.

Could Peter walk on the water? Could Jesus?

MATTHEW 14

The people were hungry. A little boy gave his lunch to Jesus. Then Jesus made it become enough for everyone. Jesus' helpers are giving the food to many, many people. Jesus can do wonderful things like that!

Who gave his lunch to Jesus? What did Jesus do with it?

JOHN 6

This woman is giving all the money she has to God's house. She is thankful for everything God has given her. She loves God and knows he will take care of her. God wants us to be thankful for all he has given us.

What can you thank God for giving you?

LUKE 21

Jesus loves children. Once some mothers brought their children to Jesus. Jesus' friends told them to go away. Jesus said, "No, let them come to me." Then Jesus held the children in his arms and loved them. Jesus loves you, too.

What did Jesus' friends say? What did Jesus say?

LUKE 18

The man on the ground was badly hurt by robbers. Several people saw him but didn't help him. Now a man has stopped and is putting bandages on his cuts. The man who helped is called the Good Samaritan. You can be a Good Samaritan by helping people.

What is the Good Samaritan doing?

LUKE 10

One day Jesus ate supper with his friends Mary and Martha. Martha was working hard to cook dinner. She was unhappy because Mary was listening to Jesus. Jesus was pleased that Mary was listening to him. What she was doing was very important.

Who was listening to Jesus?

LUKE 10

A shepherd takes good care of his sheep. He looks for them if they are lost. He picks up the lambs if they are hurt. Jesus said he is like a shepherd. We are like sheep. Even though we can't see him, we know he takes care of us.

Who is our Good Shepherd?

JOHN 10

Lazarus was one of Jesus' friends. He died, and his body was wrapped up and put into a grave in the rocks. Jesus came and prayed. Then Jesus shouted, "Lazarus, come out." At once Lazarus came back to life and came out!

What did Jesus tell Lazarus to do?

JOHN 11

The ten men in the picture were all very ill. They asked Jesus to make them well again, and he did. But only one man came back to thank Jesus. I hope you remember to say thank you when someone helps you. And always remember to say thank you to God.

How many of these men said thank you to Jesus?

This rich man asked Jesus how he could get to heaven. Jesus knew the man loved his money more than he loved God. Jesus told him to give his money away and give his life to God. To get to heaven he had to love God more than he loved his money.

What did the man love most?

LUKE 18

This father is hugging his son. His son ran away and has just come home again. He thought his father wouldn't love him anymore! But his father is very happy. God is our Father in heaven, and he is happy when we come to him.

Who is your Father in heaven?

LUKE 15

Zacchaeus climbed a tree to see Jesus. Now Jesus is talking to him. Jesus is telling him, "Come down because I am going to your house today." Zacchaeus is very glad about this. Are you glad that Jesus has come to your house?

What did Jesus tell Zacchaeus?

LUKE 19

Jesus is coming into Jerusalem riding on a donkey. The little girl is singing about how wonderful Jesus is. The fathers and mothers are waving branches to show that they are happy, too. They all want Jesus to be their new king.

What is the girl doing?

LUKE 19

Jesus is washing the feet of one of his friends. Usually big people wash their own feet. They don't like to wash other people's feet. But we should help other people, even when we don't want to.

Can you think of a time when you wanted to play, but you helped your mother instead?

JOHN 13

Jesus is eating supper with his good friends for the last time. This is called the Last Supper. He has told his friends that soon Judas will bring the soldiers to take him away. Then he will be killed. Jesus died so he can be our Saviour.

Who will take Jesus away?

LUKE 22

Jesus is praying. He knows he will soon die for our sins. He is asking God to help him. He is willing to die if that is what God wants. You and I should be like Jesus. We should always want to do what God wants us to do.

What is Jesus doing?

LUKE 22

Now something very sad is happening. Judas and the soldiers have come to get Jesus and take him away. All of Jesus' friends ran away because they were afraid. They didn't try to help him.

What did Jesus' friends do?

LUKE 22

Peter is one of Jesus' friends who ran away when the soldiers came. Now Peter is telling a lie. He says he doesn't know Jesus. He is afraid the people might hurt him for being Jesus' friend. Don't ever be afraid to tell people you love Jesus.

Why did Peter tell a lie?

LUKE 22

The soldiers have brought Jesus to a man named Pilate. Pilate can tell them to let Jesus go. But Pilate is afraid to say it. He is afraid people won't like him if he lets Jesus go. So he says, "Jesus must die."

Why was Pilate afraid to let Jesus go?

LUKE 23

They are killing Jesus. He is dying on a cross. Why are they killing him? Has he done anything wrong? No! He is dying because of the wrong things you and I have done. Jesus is letting God punish him because of our sins.

Why did Jesus die?

LUKE 23

After Jesus died, his friends put his body into a grave. Now it is Easter morning. Two women are looking into the grave. But Jesus' body isn't there! God brought Jesus back to life again, and he came out! Jesus is alive again!

Is Jesus still in the grave?

LUKE 24

After Jesus came back to life, he talked to these friends. But they didn't know it was Jesus! They were very sad because they thought Jesus was dead. Suddenly they knew he was Jesus! How happy they were to know Jesus had come back to life again!

Why were Jesus' friends sad?

LUKE 24

Look what is happening! Jesus is rising into the sky! He is going back to heaven where his Father is! He is telling his friends good-bye. But he says he will come back again. Then they will always be with him. We will be with him, too.

Where is Jesus going?

LUKE 24

Afew weeks after Jesus went back up to heaven, he sent the Holy Spirit to live in our hearts. Jesus' friends were all together. Suddenly they saw little flames on each other's heads. Can you point to them? Then the people began talking in other languages they hadn't learned!

What was on their heads?

ACTS 2

This man had never been able to walk. Even when he was a little boy he couldn't walk. But now you can see him jumping for joy. What has happened? Jesus' friends, Peter and John, told his sickness to go away! The Holy Spirit gave them this power.

What did Peter and John do?

ACTS 3

The man kneeling on the grass is Stephen. He told everyone that only Jesus could forgive their sins. He wouldn't stop telling people how wonderful Jesus is. This made the people angry. They threw rocks at him until he died and went to heaven to be with Jesus.

Why were the people angry?

ACTS 7

God sent his friend Philip to talk to the man in the chariot. Philip is telling the man about God. The man wants to be God's friend. Philip is saying he can be God's friend if he believes in Jesus. You can be God's friend, too.

What did Philip tell the man?

ACTS 8

Paul was an enemy of Jesus. He was going to hurt and kill people who believed in Jesus. Suddenly there was a bright flash of light and Paul fell down. Jesus talked to him from heaven. After that Paul told everyone that Jesus is God's Son.

Who talked to Paul from heaven?

ACTS 9

Peter is in jail for telling people that Jesus loves them and died for them. God has sent an angel to help Peter. The angel made the chains on Peter's hands and feet fall off! The doors of the jail were locked, but the angel opened them without a key, and Peter walked out.

What happened to Peter's chains?

ACTS 12

Timothy's grandmother is reading him a Bible story. When he grows up he will tell lots of people about the Bible and about Jesus. The Bible is the book God gave to us. It tells us that God loves us very much.

Do you have a Bible of your own?

2 TIMOTHY 1

Do you remember Paul? Now he is God's friend. He is leaving on a long trip in this ship. He is going to another country. He will tell people that Jesus loves them. Paul was a missionary. Perhaps you will be a missionary some day.

Where is Paul going?

ACTS 13

Paul and Silas are in jail. They are in jail because they told everyone about Jesus. But God rescued his friends. He sent a great earthquake, and their chains fell off. The doors of the jail were locked, but they flew open!

How did God rescue Paul and Silas?

ACTS 16

Paul was on a boat in a great storm. The boat sank, but God kept Paul and everyone else safe. They all swam to land. God didn't want Paul to die yet because he wanted him to be a missionary. God wanted him to tell everyone about Jesus.

What happened to the boat?

ACTS 27

Paul is in jail again. He has been there a long, long time. This time God did not send an earthquake to get him out. God still loved him just as much as ever, but he didn't rescue him. Sometimes God lets us have troubles, too. But he loves us all the time.

Where is Paul?

ACTS 28

One of Jesus' closest friends was John. When John was an old man, he had a long vision, or dream, about heaven. In his vision he saw Jesus in heaven. John wrote about what he saw. His book is called The Revelation. It is in the Bible.

Who saw heaven in a vision?

REVELATION 1

About the Author

Kenneth N. Taylor is best known as the translator of *The Living Bible*, but his first renown was as a writer of children's books. Ken and his wife, Margaret, have ten children, and his early books were written for use in the family's daily devotions. The manuscripts were ready for publication only when they passed the scrutiny of those ten young critics! Those books, which have now been read to two generations of children around the world, include *The Bible in Pictures for Little Eyes* (Moody Press), *Devotions for the Children's Hour* (Moody Press), *The Living Bible Story Book* (Tyndale House), and *Big Thoughts for Little People*, (Tyndale House). Now the Taylor children are all grown up, so *My First Bible in Pictures* was written with the numerous grandchildren in mind.

About the Illustrators

Richard and Frances Hook have produced some of this century's most beloved illustrations of Bible stories. Their style has become a standard for other contemporary illustrators. The Hooks worked together as a team, Richard illustrating the men and the backdrops, Frances the women and children.

The Hooks illustrated scores of Bible stories during their lifetimes. Tyndale House made arrangements with Concordia and Standard to reprint some of their Hook art in this book, but no Hook illustrations were available for some of the stories included in *My First Bible in Pictures*. To fill in the gaps, Tyndale House commissioned three illustrators to produce the remaining illustrations in a style reminiscent of Richard and Frances Hook's work.